# 101 Catchy Branding Slogans

Mostafa Maleki Tehrani

—F—
×
M

Firouz Media 2024

Firouz Media Limited have contributed to the
publication of this book, while the author retains
full responsibility for copyright, content accuracy,
and any legal matters. This book is a testament to
the author's commitment and enthusiasm, , and
our involvement represents a collaborative hybrid
effort in publishing. As you immerse yourself in its
contents, we sincerely hope you find inspiration,
insight, and delight.

ISBN 978-1-915557-19-3
www.firouzmedia.com
IG: @firouzmedia

Cover picture: Master1305
Stock images: Pexels_Adobe_Pixabay

***101 Catchy Branding Slogans***
Creator: Mostafa Maleki Tehrani

# Preface

Welcome to the captivating world of branding, where I invite you to join me on a journey through the annals of modern marketing. Within the pages of this compilation, I've curated 101 unforgettable slogans that have left an indelible mark on the fabric of our commercial landscape.

From the iconic simplicity of Apple's "Think Different" to the dynamic connectivity of Facebook's "Move Fast and Break Things," each slogan serves as a testament to the art of persuasion. These phrases, carefully crafted and meticulously honed, wield the power to shape perceptions, evoke emotions, and ignite passions.

Market capitalization (market cap) and brand value are two different metrics used to evaluate companies, but they both provide insights into a company's worth and potential performance. While market cap measures the overall value of a company in the stock market, brand value assesses the worth of its brand based on intangible factors like reputation and customer perception.

Here's a concise summary of their definitions and disparities:

Market Cap:
- Quantifies a company's total value in the stock market.
- Calculated by multiplying the stock price by outstanding shares.
- Reflects investor sentiment and company size.

Brand Value:
- Represents the monetary worth of a company's brand.
- Based on factors like brand recognition and customer loyalty.
- Contributes to a company's market position and competitiveness.

As you turn the pages, we'll traverse through realms of creativity and influence, gaining insight into the strategies behind some of the world's most beloved brands. Illustrated with captivating images and accompanied by invaluable market value data from the early 2024, this collection serves as both a source of inspiration and a practical guide for entrepreneurs and marketers alike. Whether you're a seasoned industry professional seeking fresh insights or an aspiring entrepreneur charting your path to success, let these slogans be our beacon. May they inspire you to craft your own memorable brand narratives and leave an enduring legacy in the world of marketing.

—Mostafa Maleki Tehrani

# 1 Think Different

Brand: Apple
Sector : Information Technology
Brand value: 880.5 billion U.S. dollars
Market cap: $2.84 Trillion

*Courtesy of Nick_H*

*Courtesy of Elisa*

# 2
## Don't be Evil

Brand: Alphabet Inc (Google)
Sector : Multinational Technology
Brand value: 577.68 billion U.S. dollars
Market cap: $1.781 Trillion

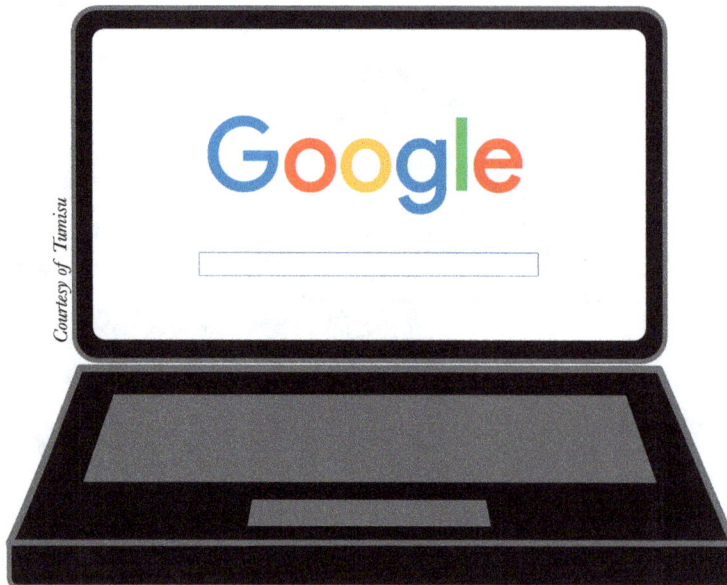
*Courtesy of Tumisu*

*Courtesy of kirstyfields*

**3** **...and You're Done**

Brand: Amazon
Sector : Retail
Brand value: 469 billion U.S. dollars
Market cap: $1.764 Trillion

Work Hard. Have Fun. Make History

*Gerd Altmann*

*Courtesy of Hitesh Sharma*

# 4 Empowering Every Person and Every Organization on the Planet

Brand: Microsoft
Sector : Information Technology
Brand value: 502 billion U.S. dollars
Market cap: $3.02 Trillion

# 5

## « It's The Real Thing »
## « Have A Coke And A Smile »
## « The Pause That Refreshes »

Brand: Coca-Cola
Sector : Beverages
Brand value: 106.1 billion U.S. dollars
Market cap: $255.81 Billion

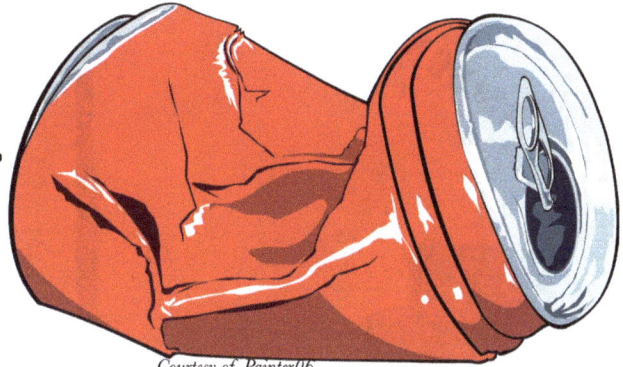

*Courtesy of Painter06*

1905 – Coca-Cola revives and sustains
1906 – The great national temperance beverage
1908 – Good til the last drop
1910 – Whenever you see an Arrow think of Coca-Cola
1917 – Three million a day
1922 – Thirst knows no season
1923 – Enjoy thirst
1924 – Refresh yourself
1925 – Six million a day
1926 – It had to be good to get where it is
1927 – Pure as Sunlight
1927 – Around the corner from anywhere
1928 – Coca-Cola ... pure drink of natural flavors
1929 – The pause that refreshes
1932 – Ice-cold sunshine
1937 – America's favorite moment
1938 – The best friend thirst ever had
1938 – Thirst asks nothing more
1939 – Coca-Cola goes along
1939 – Coca-Cola has the taste thirst goes for
1939 – Whoever you are, Whatever you do, think of good ice cold Coca-Cola.
1941 – Coca-Cola is Coke!
1942 – The only thing like Coca-Cola is Coca-Cola itself.
1944 – How about a Coke?
1945 – Coke means Coca-Cola
1945 – Passport to refreshment
1947 – Coke knows no season
1948 – Where there's Coke there's an ice cold
1949 – Coca-Cola ... along the highway to anywhere

1952 – What you want is a Coke
1954 – For people on the go
1956 – Coca-Cola ... makes good things taste better
1957 – The sign of good taste
1958 – The cold, crisp taste of Coke
1959 – Coca-Cola refreshes you best
1963 – Things go better with Coke
1969 – It's the real thing
1975 – Look up, America
1976 – Coke adds life
1979 – Have a Coke and a smile
1980 – Coke is it!
1985 – America's real choice
1986 – Red, white & you
1986 – Catch the wave
1987 – Can't beat the feeling!
1990 – Can't Beat The Real Thing
1993 – Always Coca-Cola
1995 – Always and Only Coca-Cola
1998 – Born to be red
1998 – Coca-Cola always the real thing!
1999 – Enjoy
2001 – Life tastes good
2003 – Real
2005 – Make It Real
2006 – the Coke side of life
2009–2015 – Open Happiness
2016 – Taste the Feeling
2020 – Together Tastes Better
2020 – Be Open Like Never Before

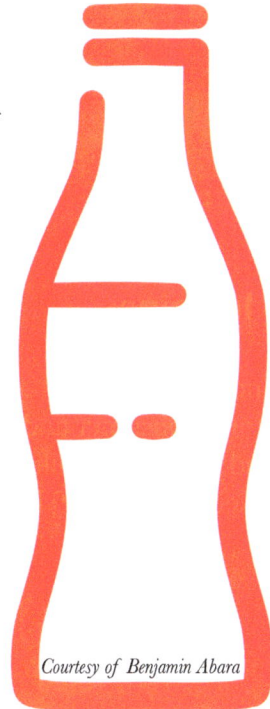

*Courtesy of Benjamin Abara*

SAMSUNG

Courtesy of Katherine Gomez

# 6 Imagine

Brand: Samsung
Sector : Consumer and industry electronics
Brand value: 91.4 billion U.S. dollars
Market cap: $376.39 billion

"Inspire The World, Create The Future"
"Imagine The Possibilities"
"Samsung Is Rising"
"The Next Is Now"
"Unleash The Power Of Your Every Side"

Courtesy of FineFlowersForFamilyFirst

# 7 LET`S GO PLACES

Brand: Toyota
Sector : Automotive
Brand value: 64. 5 billion U.S. dollars
Market cap: $308.16 Billion

You asked for it, You got it! (1975–1979)
Oh what a feeling! (1979–1985)
Who could ask for anything more? (1985–1989)
I love what you do for me (1989–1997)
Everyday (1997–2001)
Get The Feeling (2001–2004)
Moving Forward (2004–2012)

*Courtesy of Sunny Daye*

# *8* The Best or Nothing

Brand: Mercedes-Benz
Sector : Automotive
Brand value: 61 billion U.S. dollars
Market cap: $1.7 Trillion

**9** **It's time to build**

*If you think we're not good for your business, leave*

"More Together"

Brand: Meta Platforms (Facebook)
Sector : Social network service, advertising, and business insight solutions
Brand value: 59 billion U.S. dollars
Market cap: $1.233 Trillion

# 10

## I'm Lovin' It

Brand: McDonald's
Sector : Consumer Discretionary
Brand value: 191.11 billion U.S. dollars
Market cap: $210.76 Billion

*Courtesy of Grafikaesky*

"Go off and do something wonderful"

*Courtesy of mickdahl*

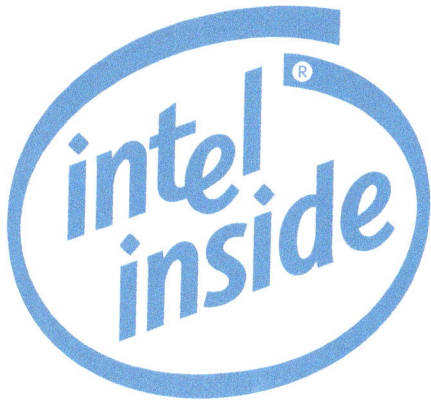

"Sponsors of tomorrow"

# 11 Intel inside

Brand: Intel
Sector : Semiconductor & Circuit Manufacturer
Brand value: 31.8 billion U.S. dollars
Market cap: $186.24 Billion

# 12 THINK

Brand: IBM
Sector : Information technology products and services
Brand value: 10.6 billion U.S. dollars
Market cap: $170.63 Billion

THINK.

I think therefore IBM.

We Make IT Happen.

Solutions for a small planet.

Computers help people help people.

# 13 Sheer Driving Pleasure

Brand: BMW
Sector : Manufacturer of premium cars and motorcycles
Brand value: 20.94 billion U.S. dollars
Market cap: $72.68 Billion

Bernardsie

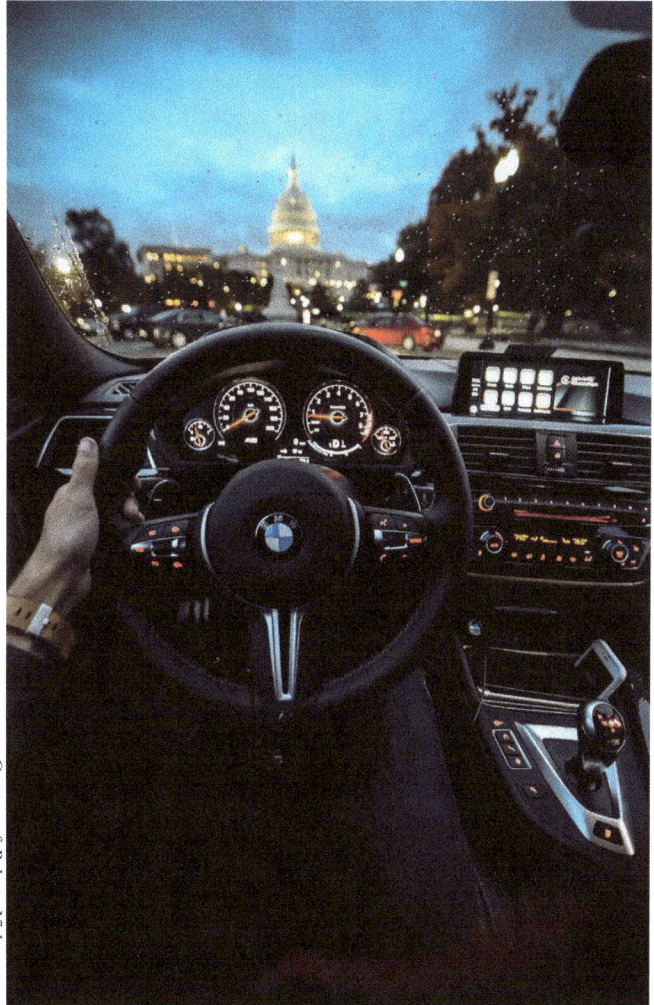

Courtesy of Roberto Nickson

# 14

## The Happiest Place on Earth

Brand: Disney
Sector : Media entertainment industry
Brand value: 57.06 billion U.S. dollars
Market cap: $206.26 Billion

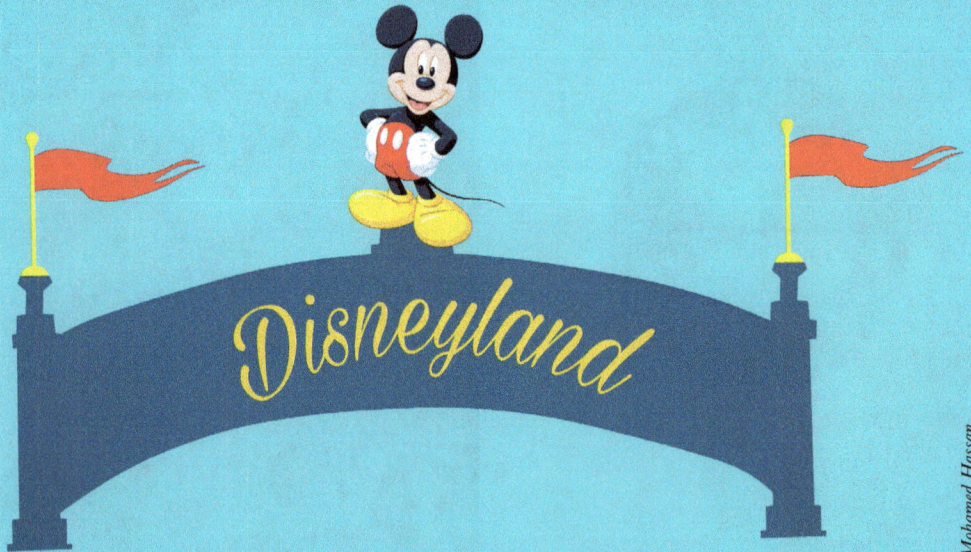

*Courtesy of Mohamed Hassan*

**This is the Power of the Network. Now.**

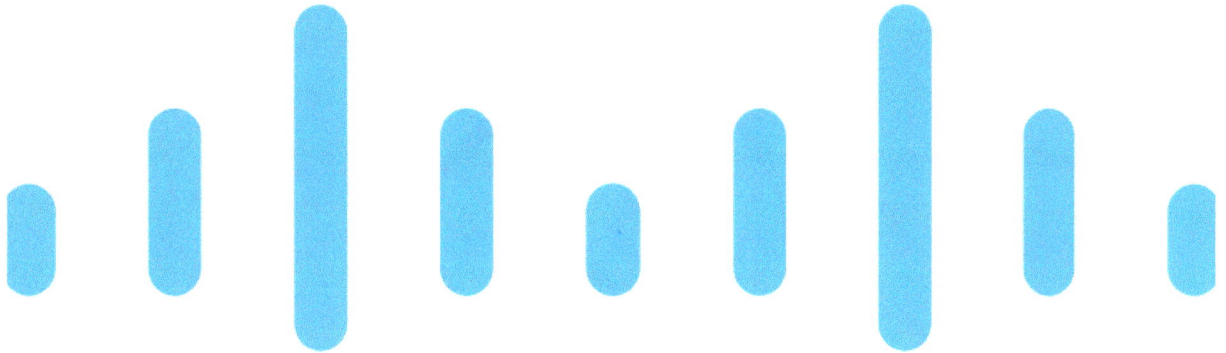

# CISCO

## 15 The Bridge to Possible

Brand: Cisco
Sector : Computer Communications Equipment
Brand value: 21.3 billion U.S. dollars
Market cap: $204.31 Billion

# Building a World That Works

# 16

## We Bring Good Things to Life

Brand: General Electric (GE)
Sector : Diversified High-tech Industrial
(aerospace, power, renewable energy, digital
industry, additive manufacturing, and venture
capital and finance)
Brand value: 37.2 billion U.S. dollars
Market cap: $161.50 Billion

*Courtesy of Samuel Jiménez*

# 17 **Just Do It**

Brand: Nike
Sector : Athletic & Sporting Goods Manufacturer
Brand value: 30 billion U.S. dollars
Market cap: $160.67 Billion

Courtesy of Tarek Shahin

# 18
## L.V the Truth

Brand: Louis Vuitton
Sector : Luxury Goods
Brand value: 124.8 billion U.S. dollars
Market cap: $439.89 Billion

*Courtesy of Pratik Prasad*

# 19 Love Your Curves

Brand: Zara
Sector : Apparel and Personal Care
Brand value: 16.5 billion U.S. dollars
Market cap: 132.49 Billion

*You meet the nicest people on a Honda*

## 20 Power of Dreams

Brand: Honda
Sector : Automotive and Power Equipment Manufacturer
Brand value: 22.696 billion U.S. dollars
Market cap: $54.68 Billion

*Courtesy of Freddy*

**Helping the World Run Better**

# SAP

## 21
### The Best Run SAP

Brand: SAP
Sector : Technical and Business Services
(Provider of Enterprise Software, Business Solutions,
Cloud Computing, and Consulting Services)
Brand value: 55.6 billion U.S. dollars
Market cap: $207.27 Billion

1939–1950: "Twice as Much for a Nickel"
1950: "More Bounce to the Ounce"
1950–1957: "Any Weather is Pepsi Weather"
1957–1958: "Say Pepsi, Please"
1961–1964: "Now It's Pepsi for Those Who Think Young"
1964–1967: "Come Alive, You're in the Pepsi Generation"
1967–1969: "(Taste that beats the others cold) Pepsi Pours It On".
1969–1975: "You've Got a Lot to Live, and Pepsi's Got a Lot to Give"
1977–1980: "Join the Pepsi People (Feeling Free)"
1980–1981: "Catch That Pepsi Spirit"
1981–1983: "Pepsi's got your taste for life"
1983–1984: "Pepsi Now! Take the Challenge!"
1984–1988 and 1990-1991: "Pepsi. The Choice of a New Generation"
1989: "Pepsi. A Generation Ahead"
1991–1992: "Gotta Have It"/"Chill Out"
1992: "The Choice Is Yours"
1992–1993: "Be Young, Have Fun, Drink Pepsi"
1993–1994: "Right Now"
1994–1995: "Double Dutch Bus"
1995: "Nothing Else is a Pepsi"
1995–1996: "Drink Pepsi. Get Stuff"
1996: "Change The Script"
1997–1998: "Generation Next"
1998–1999: "It's the cola" (100th anniversary commercial)
1999–2000: "For Those Who Think Young"/"The Joy of Pepsi-Cola"
2003: "Its the Cola"/"Dare for More"
2006–2007: "Why You Doggin' Me"/"Taste the one that's forever young"
2007–2008: "More Happy"/"Taste the one that's forever young"
2008: "Pepsi is #1"
2008–present: "Something For Everyone"
2009–present: "Refresh Everything"/"Every Generation Refreshes the World"
2010–present: "Every Pepsi Refreshes The World"
2011–present: "Summer Time is Pepsi Time"
2011–present: "Born in the Carolinas"
2012: "Where there's Pepsi, there's music" – used for the 2012 Super Bowl commercial
2012: "Live For Now"
2012: "Change The Game"
2012: "The Best Drink Created Worldwide"

# 22
## Rise Up, Baby!

Brand: Pepsi
Sector : Beverages
Brand value: 18 billion U.S. dollars
Market cap: $230.71 Billion

# 23

## To be irreplaceable, one must be different

Brand: Chanel
Sector : Fashion
Brand value: 56 billion U.S. dollars
Market cap: $440 Billion

A girl should be two things: Classy & Fabulous

Share the fantasy.

# 24 Don't Leave Home Without It

Brand: American Express
Sector: Financial Services
Brand value: 60.5 billion U.S. dollars
Market cap: $153.84 Billion

# **25** Complete. Open. Integrated

Brand: Oracle
Sector: Information Technology
(Enterprise software, Business software, Cloud computing)
Brand value: 91,992 billion U.S. dollars
Market cap: $310.02 Billion

- Information driven.
- No 1 database in the world.
- Can't break it, can't break-in.
- Software Powers the Internet.
- Enabling the Information Age.
- Mobile data management platform.
- Fastest ever database performance.
- Runs faster. Costs less. And never breaks.
- The Information Company.
- Software. Hardware. Complete.
- Hardware and Software, Engineered to Work Together.
- Integrated Cloud Applications and Platform Services.
- A complete enterprise cloud designed to modernize your business.

# 26
## First-Class Business… in a First-Class Way

Brand: J.P. Morgan
Sector : Financial Services and Investment Banking
Brand value: 30.1 billion U.S. dollars
Market cap: $520.01 Billion

# 27 To create a better everyday life for the many people

Brand: IKEA
Sector: Furniture and furnishing products
Brand value: 15.93 billion U.S. dollars

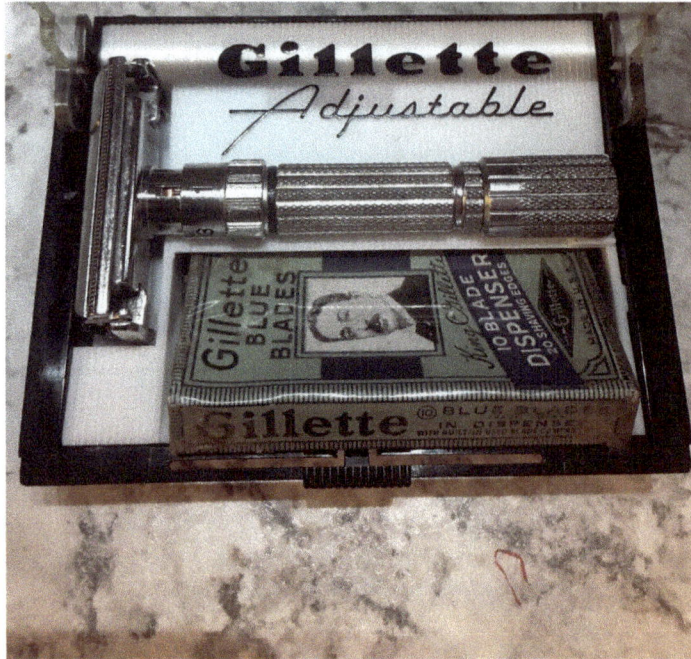

## **28** **The Best A Man Can Be**

Brand: Gillette
Sector: Personal Care Products Manufacturer.
Fast-Moving Consumer Goods (FMCG)
Brand value: 6.6 billion U.S. dollars
Market cap: $217.79 Billion

# **29** What can brown do for you?

Brand: UPS
Sector: Logistics/ Delivery Services
Brand value: 38.5 billion U.S. dollars
Market cap: $125.22 Billion

## 30 Brighter than ever

Brand: H&M
Sector: Retail (fashion and design)
Brand value: 19.2 billion U.S. dollars
Market cap: $204.87 Billion

Checked out.
Be conscious.
Long live fashion.
Look for the M on every piece.
Go green wear blue.
Reality is better than fantasy.
Hate and Merchandise.
The makers of happy and merry.
Continue in style.
We save the rain.
Soak up the sun in exotic prints and style.
Fashion in context.
The new looks.
White holidays.
My passion for fashion.
Get ready to do some serious shopping.
Beckham for HM.
Pride is always.
The wait is over H&M sale is on.
Meet H&M Stylist.
Stay stylish and warm.
Going green in black is possible.
Feel at home.
You look nice today.

*Courtesy of Nataliya Vaitkevich*

**Pampers**

- Love, sleep & play.

- Peaceful nights. Playful days.

- Inspired by babies. Created by Pampers.

- Discover your baby's world at pampers.com

## 31 Peaceful nights. Playful days.

Brand: Pampers
Sector: Baby and Toddler Care (FMCG)
Brand value: 13.8 billion U.S. dollars

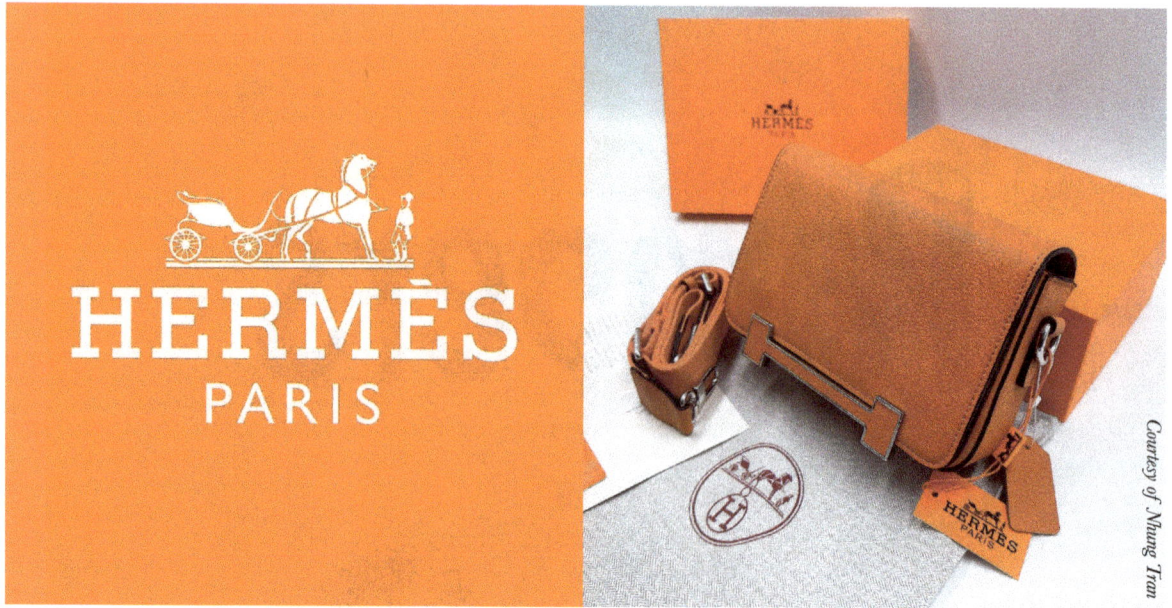

*Courtesy of Nhung Tran*

## 32  You dream it up Hermes makes it happen

Brand: Hermes
Sector: Luxury Goods
Brand value: 30.2 billion U.S. dollars
Market cap: $233.75 Billion

Father Christmas won't bring you anything – Hermes will

The first step in the new century
Simply Hermes — ing
The parcel people

# 33 SOMETHING MORE THAN BEER

Brand: Budweiser
Sector: Alcohol
Brand value: 13 billion U.S. dollars
Market cap: $124.67 Billion

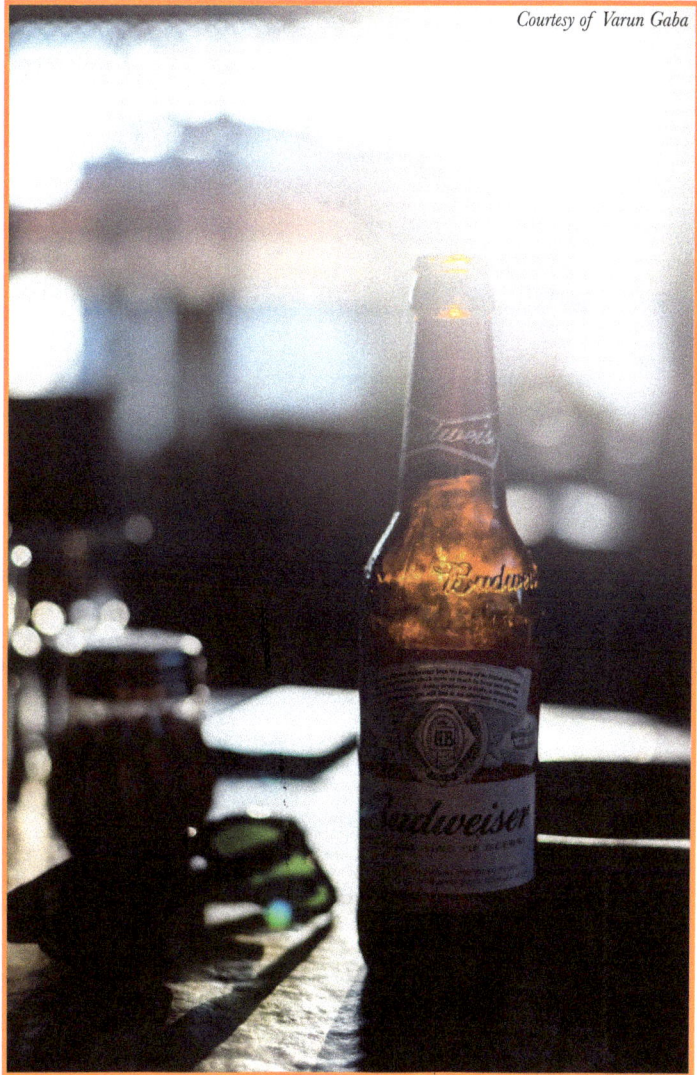

*Courtesy of Varun Gaba*

"THE KING OF BEERS."

"SHE FOUND, SHE MARRIED TWO MEN."

"SHE FOUND, SHE HAS IT ALL."

"WHERE THERE'S LIFE… THERE'S BUD."

GOOD TIMES. BAD TIMES. EXTRA TIMES.

# 34 Let there be change

Brand: Accenture
Sector: Business Services
(Information Technology Consulting)
Brand value: 40.5 billion U.S. dollars
Market cap: $247.62 Billion

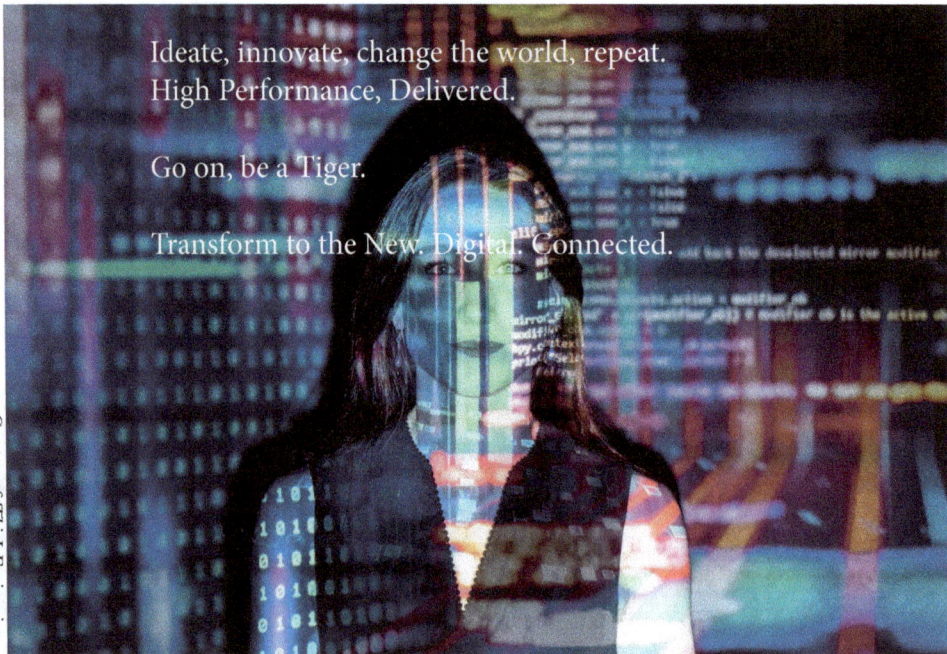

Ideate, innovate, change the world, repeat.
High Performance, Delivered.

Go on, be a Tiger.

Transform to the New. Digital. Connected.

*Courtesy of ThisIsEngineering*

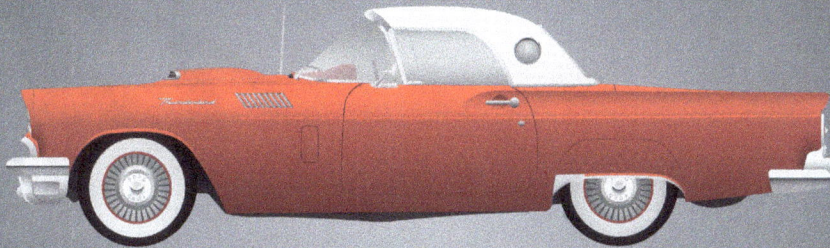

*Courtesy of Pixabay*

# 35 **Built Ford Tough**

Brand: Ford
Sector: Automotive
Brand value: 13.21 billion U.S. dollars
Market cap: $49.75 Billion

*Courtesy of Erik Mclean*

## 36

**New thinking, New possibilities**

Brand: Hyundai
Sector: Automotive
Brand value: 20.4 billion U.S. dollars
Market cap: 63.61 Trillion KRW

# 37

## Bring out the best in you

Brand: NESCAFE
Sector: Beverages
Brand value: 22.4 billion U.S. dollars
Market cap: 259.47 Billion CHF

*It all starts with a Nescafé.*

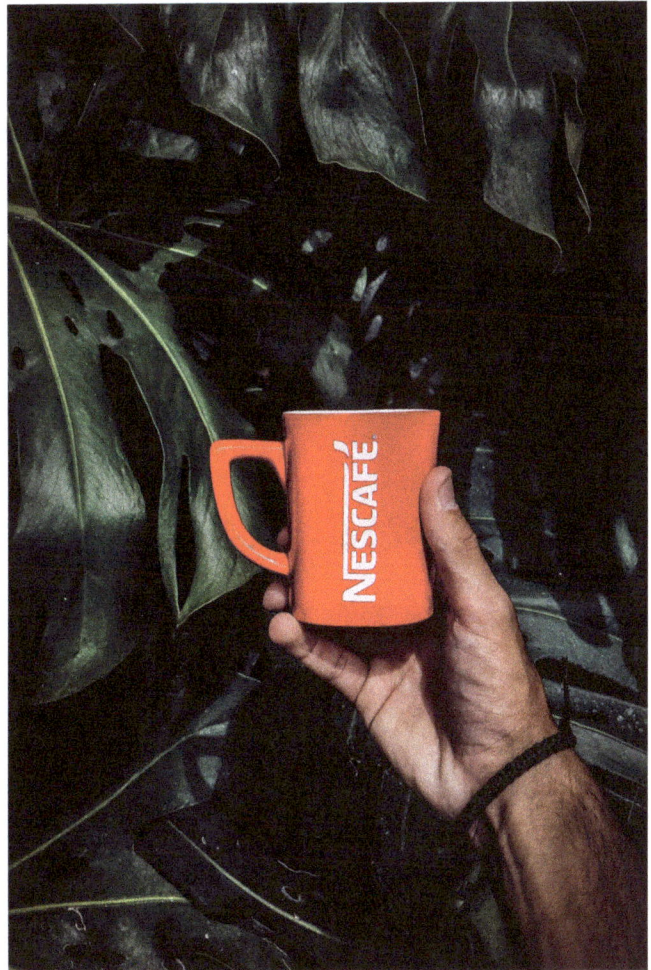

Courtesy of Aditya Aiyar

Whatever it is you're looking for, do it on eBay. (2004)

The power of all of us. (2005)

Whatever it is. (2005)

You can get it on ebay. (2006)

Whatever it is you can get it on eBay. (2006)

Shop victoriously. (2007)

Come to think of it, ebay. (2009)

Shop the world. (2014)

Fill your cart with color. (2017)

Buy it. Sell it. Love it

# **38** The World's Online Market Place

Brand: eBay Inc
Sector: E-Commerce Marketplace
Brand Revenue: 9.795 billion U.S. dollars
Market cap: $22.12 Billion

# 39 Quality is Remembered Long After the Price is Forgotten

Brand: Gucci
Sector: Luxury Fashion
Brand value: 17.8 billion U.S. dollars

GUCCI

Courtesy of Anastasia Shuraeva

*Courtesy of Julius H.*

**NISSAN**
*innovation that excites*

**40** **Life is a journey. Enjoy the ride.**

Brand: Nissan
Sector: Automotive
Brand value: 11 billion U.S. dollars
Market cap: 2.23 Trillion JPY

*Courtesy of Lil artsy*

# 41
## Drivers Wanted
## Think Small

Brand: Volkswagen
Sector: Automotive
Brand value: 21 billion U.S. dollars
Market cap: 64.77 Billion EUR

Powered by Nature

# 42

## Progress Through Technology

Brand: Audi
Sector: Automotive (Automobile Manufacturer)
Brand value: $17,187 million U.S. dollars
Market cap: $82.99 Billion

*Courtesy of Alexander Pollinger*

- Innovation plus you
- More light more magic
- Light us
  Now smart is simple
- Perfect if you have a bit of Italian stuck between your teeth
- Reveal your skin's natural radiance
- What makes LED light the smarter brighter choice
  Change the world. One bulb at a time
- Switch to a light that's easier on your eyes
- Reveal more
- Stay picture-perfect all summer holidays
- You feel different
- Building an interactive web experience
- Stay picture-perfect all summer holidays

**PHILIPS**

# 43 Together, we make life better

Brand: Philips
Sector: Electronics (Health Technology)
Brand value: 12.8 billion U.S. dollars
Market cap: 17.19 Billion EUR

*Courtesy of G.C.*

# 44 Progress is Everyone's Business

Brand: Goldman Sachs
Sector: Financial Services
Brand value: 16.40 billion U.S. dollars
Market cap: $125.69 Billion

![citigroup logo]

# 45 Citi – Never Sleeps.

Brand: Citigroup Inc
Sector: Financial Services and Investment Banking
Brand value: 34.4 billion U.S. dollars
Market cap: $105.07 Billion

Memed_Nurrohmad

Courtesy of Colin Behrens

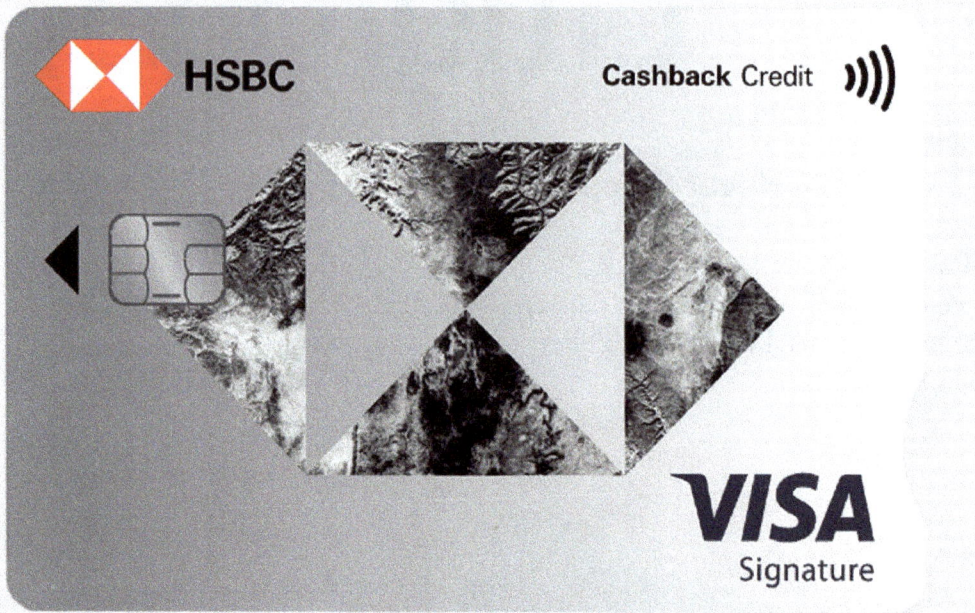

# 46
## The World's Local Bank

Brand: HSBC
Sector: Financial Services
Brand value: 16.71 billion U.S. dollars
Market cap: $121.12 Billion

# **47** **Know You Can**

Brand: AXA
Sector: Insurance Company
Brand value: 15.9 billion U.S. dollars
Market cap: 70.33 Billion EUR

# 48

## Because You`re Worth it

Brand: L`Oreal
Sector: Beauty and Personal Care (FMCG)
Brand value: 38 billion U.S. dollars
Market cap: 236.94 Billion EUR

# 49
## Caringly Yours

Brand: Allianz
Sector: Insurance and Asset Management
Brand value: 20 billion U.S. dollars
Market cap: 97.62 Billion EUR

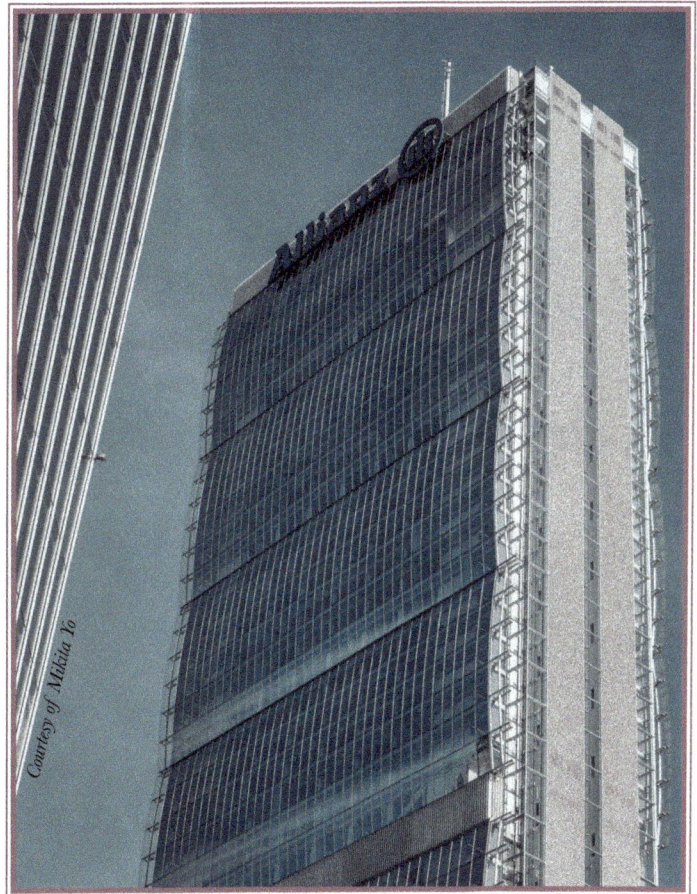

- The Complexity of Simplicity.
- Protects You From A-Z.
- You can trust Allianz.
- The Power on Your Side.
- Be sure, not just insured.
- Insurance solutions from A to Z.
- For all that's ahead.
- Take the next step.

Courtesy of Mikita Io

# 50

## Impossible Is Nothing

Brand: Adidas
Sector: Textile and Footwear
Brand value: 16 billion U.S. dollars
Market cap: 32.04 Billion EUR

*Courtesy of Paul Voie*

*ALL in or Nothing*

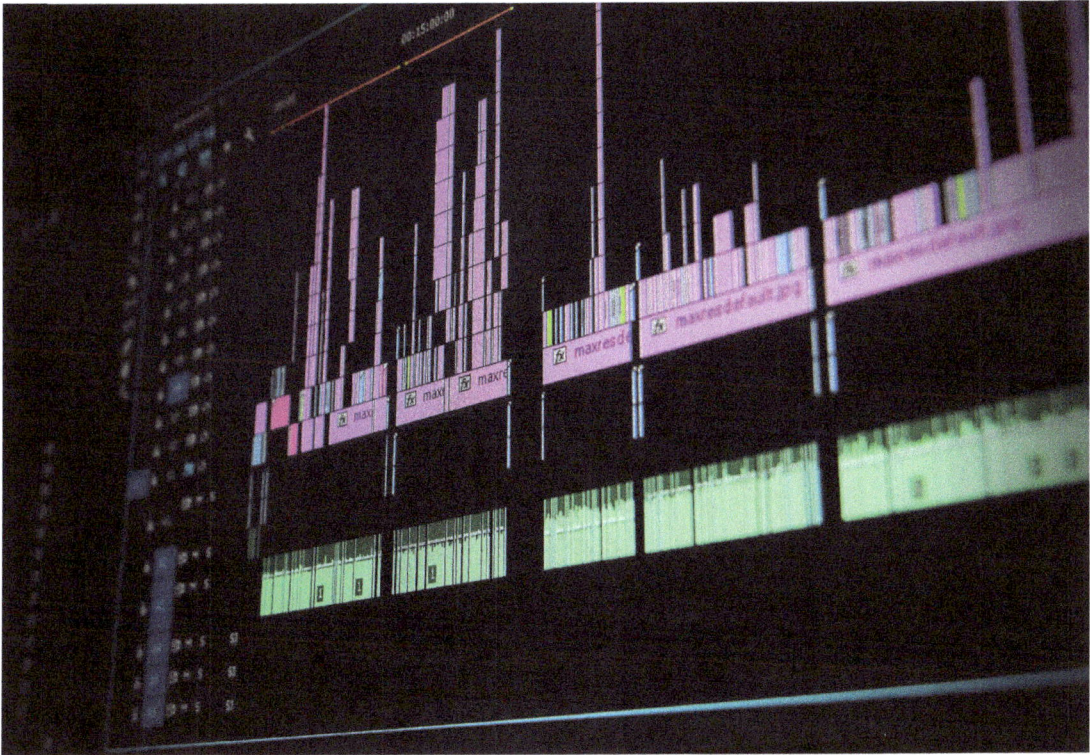

# 51 Better by Adobe

Brand: Adobe Inc
Sector: Design Software and Online Sales
Brand value: 92.83 billion U.S. dollars
Market cap: $266.88 Billion

Courtesy of Pixabay

# **52** There is no subsitute

Brand: Porsche
Sector: Automotive
Brand value: 16.2 billion U.S. dollars
Market cap: 36.72 Billion EUR

# 53 They're GR-R-R-reat

Brand: Kellogg`s
Sector: Food processing (FMCG)
Brand value: 7 billion U.S. dollars
Market cap: $18.97 Billion

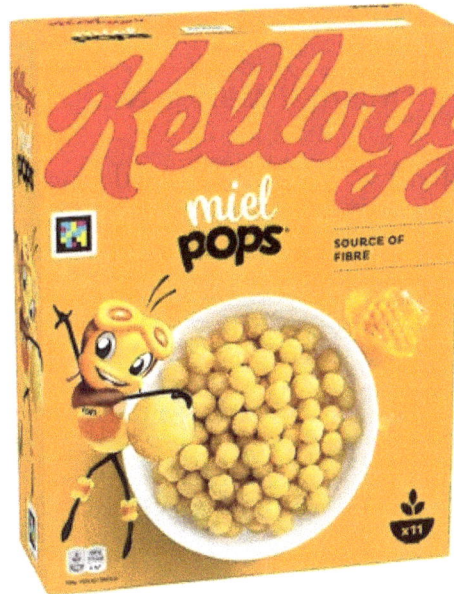

Grow With Us.
Kellogg's puts more into your day.
Let's Make Today Great.
Pick a ripe box today.
The simpler the better.
The Best To You Each Morning…from Kellogg's.
Fruit and Fibre. Tastes so good, you'll forget the fiber..
L'eggo my Eggo!
Pop-Tarts. Crazy good.
Because that's the kind of Mom you are.
The simpler the better.

# 54
## Make it Matter Keep Reinventing

Brand: HP (Hewlett Packard Enterprise)
Sector: Technology Products and Solutions
Brand value: 30 billion U.S. dollars
Market cap: $28.77 Billion

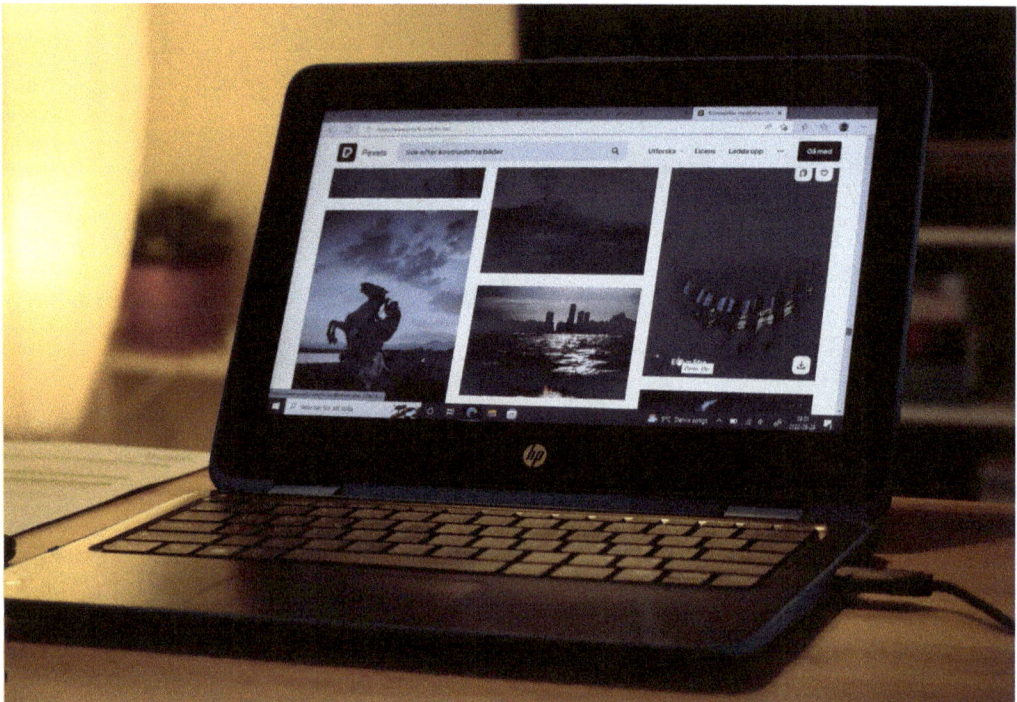

*Courtesy of Damir*

# 55
## Delighting You Always

Brand: Canon
Sector: Imaging and Optical Products
Brand value: 27.62 billion U.S. dollars
Market cap: 5.60 Trillion JPY

**Canon**

*Courtesy of Kiên Trịnh*

# **56** Ingenuity for life

Brand: Siemens
Sector: Industrial Conglomerates
(buildings, electrification, and electrical products)
Brand value: 21.6 billion U.S. dollars
Market cap: 135.04 Billion EUR

*Courtesy of Dmboch*

# 57 Coffee and more

Brand: Starbucks
Sector: Food and Beverage
Brand value: 53.4 billion U.S. dollars
Market cap: $105.54 Billion

To inspire and nurture the human spirit—one person, one cup and one neighborhood at a time.

Courtesy of Tansholpan

## 58 Danone, One Planet. One Health

Brand: Danone
Sector: Food and Beverage (FMCG)
Brand value: 9 billion U.S. dollars
Market cap: 41.32 Billion EUR

# 59 make.believe

Brand: Sony
Sector: Electronics
Brand value: 113.20 billion U.S. dollars
Market cap: 17 Trillion JPY

*Courtesy of Gift Habeshaw*

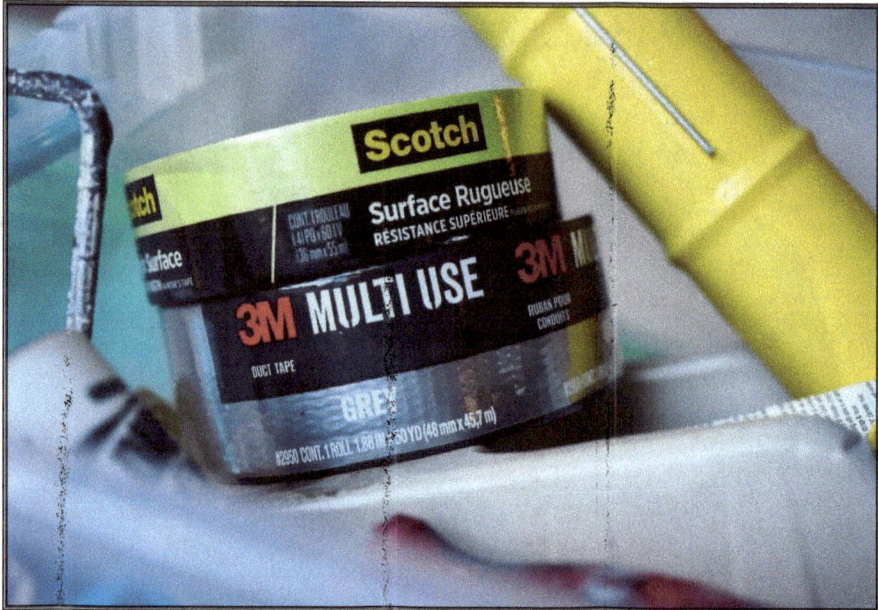

Mistake = Magic = Money

**3M Science. Applied to Life.™**

# 60 Science. Applied to Life

Brand: 3M
Sector: Diversified Technology Services (Safety and Industrial;
Transportation and Electronics; Health Care; and Consumer)
Brand value: 9.79 billion U.S. dollars
Market cap: $50.65 Billion

# 61 It`s everywhere you want to be

Brand: Visa Inc
Sector: Payment Technology
Brand value: 169.1 billion U.S. dollars
Market cap: $562.75 Billion

Courtesy of Profoundeos

# 62

## The Good food, Good life company

Brand: Nestle
Sector: Food and Beverage (FMCG)
Brand value: 22.4 billion U.S. dollars
Market cap: 260.06 Billion CHF

Courtesy of Steve Buissinne

# 63
## World Wise

Brand: Morgan Stanley
Sector: Financial Services
Brand value: 290.96 billion U.S. dollars
Market cap: $141.22 Billion

*Gordon Johnson*

Morgan Stanley

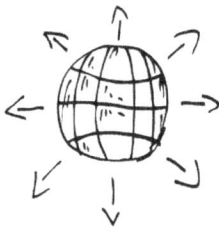

*Courtesy of Jozef Mikulcik*

# 64 Stronger, healthier gums.

Brand: Colgate
Sector: Personal Care and Oral Hygiene (FMCG)
Market cap: $69.30 Billion

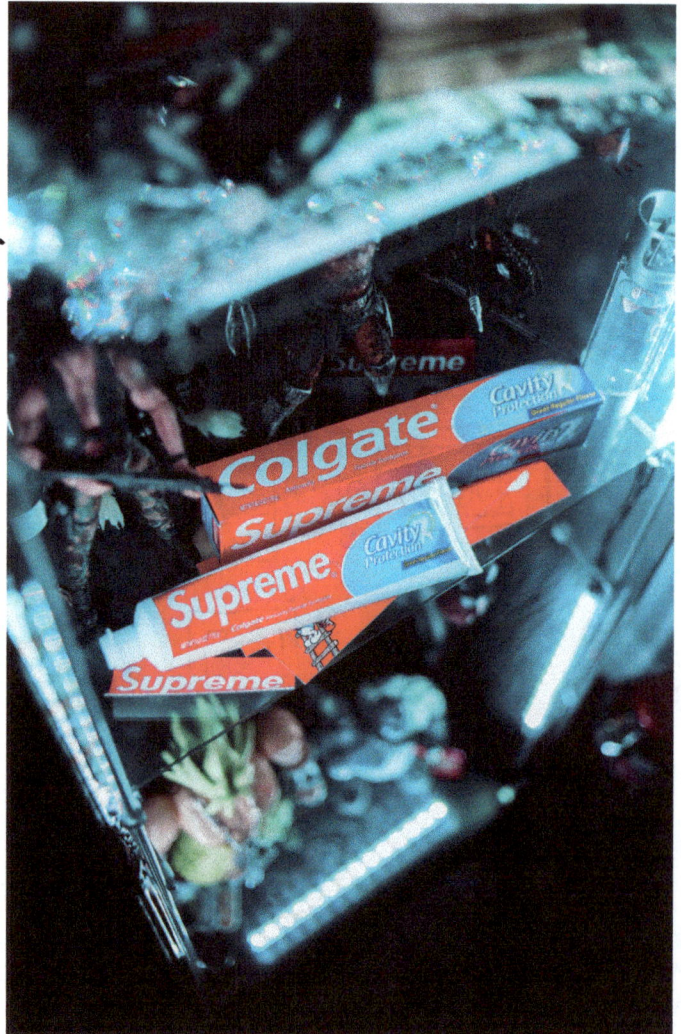

*Courtesy of Erik Mclean*

- It stays on the job fighting cavities.
- For superstars like you.

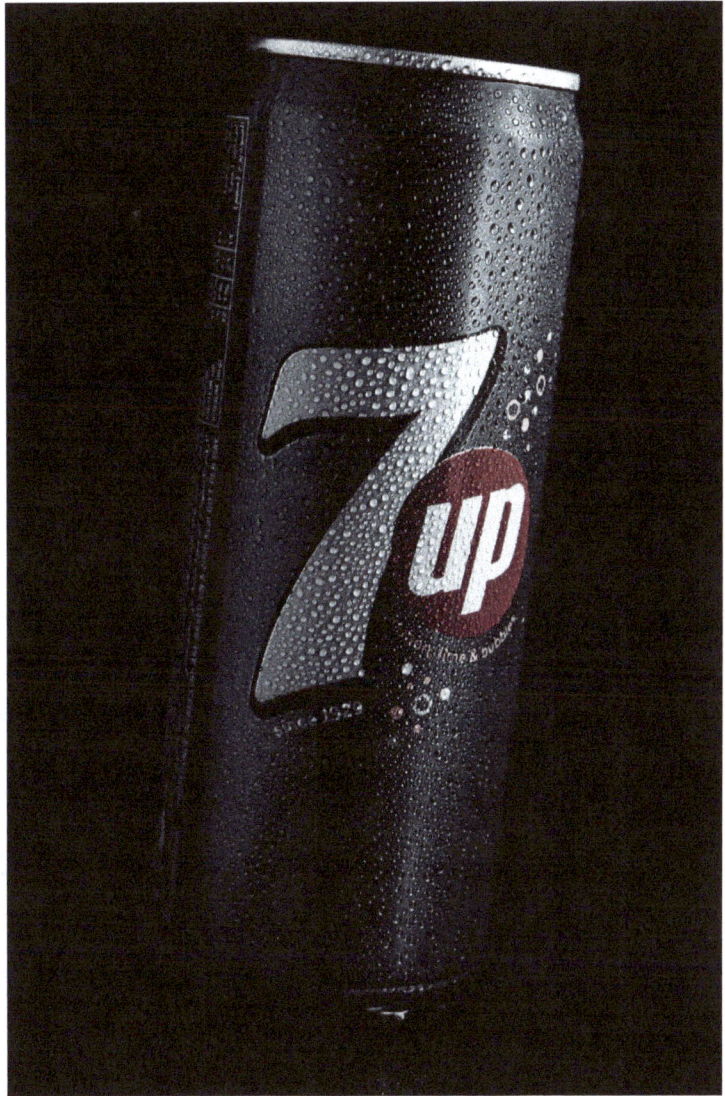

*Courtesy of Youssef Samuil*

# 65 The Uncola

Brand: 7up
Sector: Beverage and Soft Drinks
Market cap: 2.16 Billion THB
Ridiculously Bubbly. Be yourself. Be refreshing
New Get Up, Same 7UP

# 66
## Love

Brand: Subaru
Sector: Automotive
Brand value: 16.61 billion U.S. dollars
Market cap: 2.50 Trillion JPY

*Courtesy of Johnny_px*

How far would you go for Love?

# 67
## True love has a color and name

Brand: Cartier
Sector: Luxury Goods
Brand value: 12.5 billion U.S. dollars
Market cap: 73.34 Billion CHF

Think in pink.
Cartier affair.
Cartier time art.
A year of Cartier.
Case by Csrtier.
Paris Paris Paris.
The Cartier's hope.
Etourdissant Cartier.
Les must de Cartier.
The Art of Being Unique.
Inde Mysteriesue collection.
The newest must from Paris.
Never imitate, always innovate.
How far would you go for Love?
Magnitude high jewellery Cartier.
True love has a color and a name.
The queen of bling size does matter.
Pearl's collection - Cartier classic jewellery.
It has been there for decades - Cartier pure gold.

*Courtesy of Cartier*

**68**

## Make it possible

Brand: Huawei
Sector: Information and Communications Technology
Brand value: 44 billion U.S. dollars
Market cap: $1.3 Trillion

# 69
## Here to help you prosper

Brand: Banco Santander
Sector: Financial Services
Brand Revenue: 11.08 billion U.S. dollars
Market cap: 58 Billion EUR

*Courtesy of Mireya Fernandez*

# 70

## There Are Some Things Money Can't Buy. For Everything Else, There's MasterCard

Brand: Mastercard
Sector : Financial Services (global payments industry)
Market cap: $438.78 Billion

# 71

## Movement that inspires

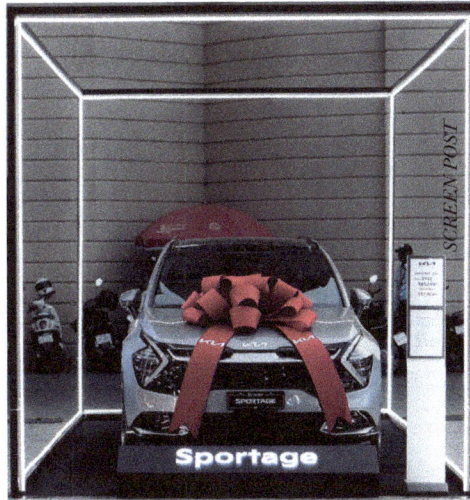

Brand: Kia
Sector : Automotive
Brand value: 34.36 billion U.S. dollars
Market cap: 46.27 Trillion KRW

# 72

## When It Absolutely, Positively Has To Be There Overnight

Brand: FedEx
Sector: Logistics and Transportation
Brand value: 28.9 billion U.S. dollars
Market cap: $59.37 Billion

The World on Time

Courtesy of Mike Shinzo

# 73

## Because You Have To

Brand: PayPal
Sector: Financial Technology (FinTech)
Market cap: $63.38 Billion

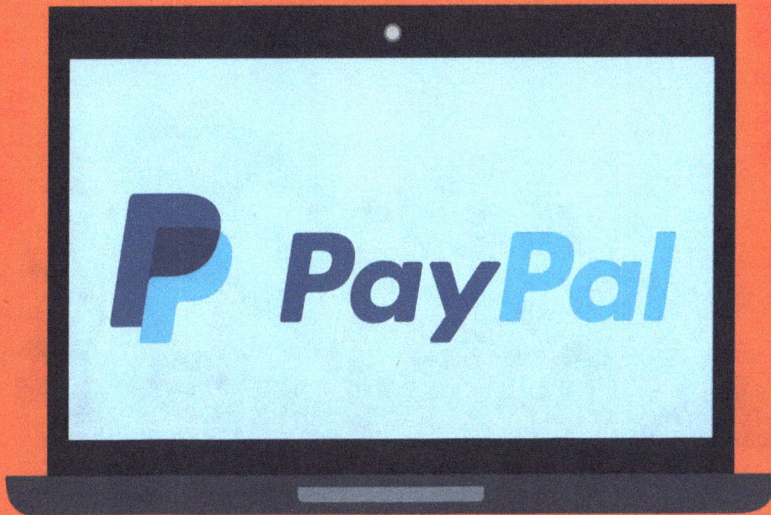

*Courtesy of Mohamed Hassan*

# **74** Only the Best is Good Enough

Brand: LEGO
Sector: Toys
Brand value: 7.4 billion U.S. dollars

*Courtesy of Francis Ray*

## 75 Bringing people together changes everything.

Brand: Salesforce
Sector: Cloud Computing and Customer Relationship Management (CRM)
Market cap: $280.45 Billion

## 76 Live Your Best

Brand: Panasonic
Sector: Consumer Electronics and Technology
Brand value: 21.57 billion U.S. dollars
Market cap: 3.48 Trillion JPY

Ideas for Life

Wojciech Magdziak vel Wierzbicki

# *11* Your Druggist is More Than a Merchant

Brand: Johnson & Johnson
Sector: Healthcare Products, Pharmaceutical and MedTech (FMCG)
Brand value: 14 billion U.S. dollars
Market cap: $376.86 Billion

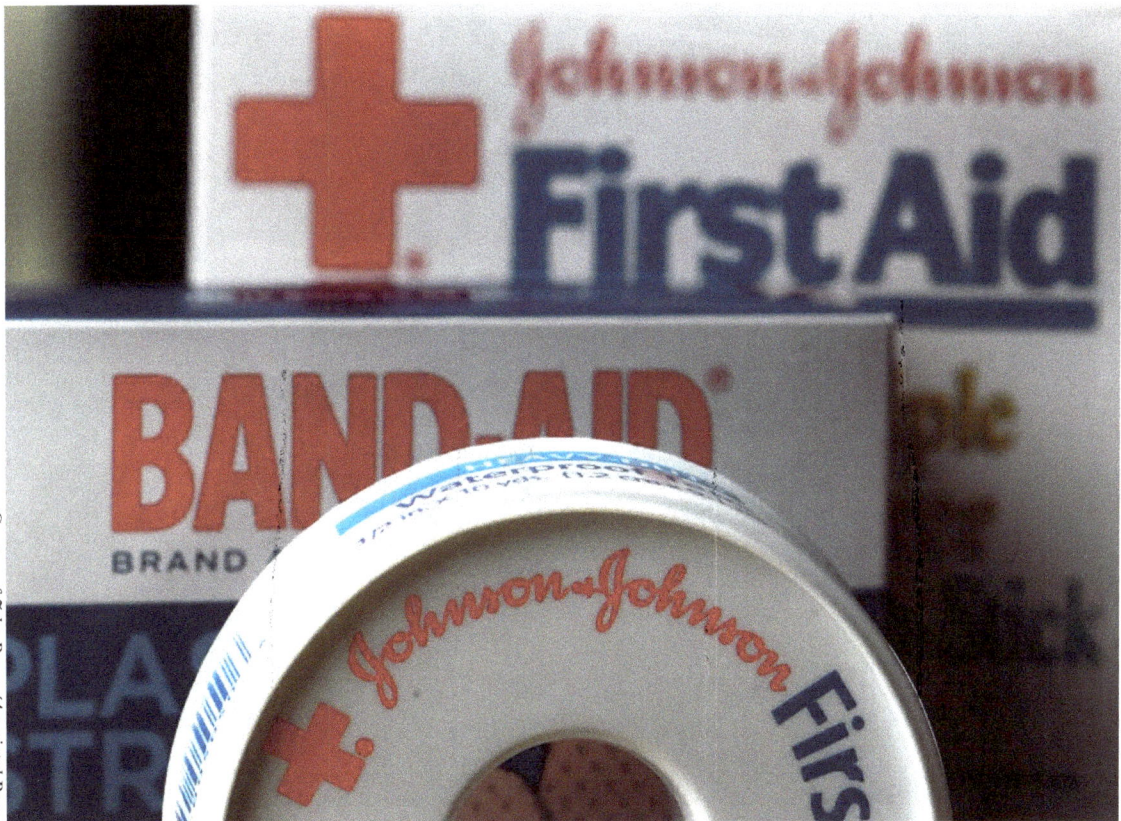

# 78

## Above and Beyond

Brand: Land Rover
Sector: Automotive
Brand value: 4.47 billion U.S. dollars
Market cap: $1.7 Trillion

*Courtesy of Ahmad Syahrir*

# 79

## We move the world.

Brand: DHL
Sector: Logistics
Brand value: 6 billion U.S. dollars
Market cap: $50.47 Billion

# *80* We are the competition.

Brand: Ferrari
Sector: Automotive
Brand value: 9.2 billion U.S. dollars
Market cap: 70.30 Billion EUR

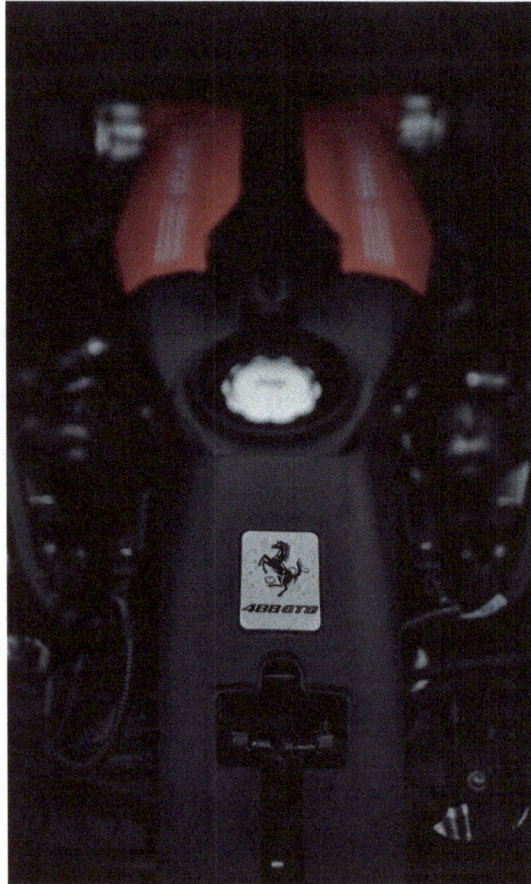

*Courtesy of Zachary DeBottis*

# 81 There's No Thrill Like Discovery. Entertain Your Brain.

Brand: Discovery
Sector: Media and Entertainment
Brand value: 1.38 billion U.S. dollars
Market cap: $23.97 Billion

The world is ours. Explore Your World.

# 82 LET'S DO THE WORK™

Brand: Caterpillar
Sector: Diversified
(Heavy Machinery and Equipment Manufacturing
Brand value: 8.065 million U.S. dollars

Courtesy of Caterpillar

# 83

## TRUE LOVE GROWS

Brand: Tiffany & Co.
Sector: Luxury Goods and Jewelry
Brand value: 7 billion U.S. dollars

Courtesy of Mariya B.

# 84 Make it Count

Brand: Jack Daniels
Sector: Manufacturing and distillation of liquors
Brand value: 7.171 billion U.S. dollars
Market cap: $27.81 Billion

*Courtesy of Oli P*

# 85 Miles Away From ordinary

Brand: Corona
Sector: Alcohol (Beer)
Brand value: 7 billion U.S. dollars
Market cap:  $28.29 Billion

# 86 Finger Lickin' Good

Brand: KFC
Sector: Fast Food Restaurant
Brand value: 6.09 billion U.S. dollars
Market cap: $37.81 Billion

# 87 Open Your World

Brand: Heineken
Sector: Beverage and Alcohol
Brand value: 7.6 billion U.S. dollars
Market cap: 52.02 Billion EUR

Courtesy of John Deere

# 88
## Nothing Runs Like A Deere

Brand: John Deere
Sector: Agricultural Machinery and Equipment Manufacturer
Brand value: 8.1 billion U.S. dollars
Market cap: $100.99 Billion

# 89 You can be sure of Shell.

Brand: Shell
Sector: Energy and Oil & Gas
Brand value: 48.2 billion U.S. dollars
Market cap: 161.58 Billion GBP

'Go Well – Go Shell'.

# 90

## It's a MINI adventure

Brand: MINI
Sector: Automotive
Brand value: 5 billion U.S. dollars
Márket cap: $30.5 Billion

**MINI**

*Small Wins*

*Courtesy of The Lazy Artist Gallery*

*Courtesy of Tiểu Bảo Trương*

# 91
## We Should All Be Feminists

Brand: Dior
Sector: Luxury Goods and Fashion
Brand value: 9.7 billion U.S. dollars
Market cap: 143.53 Billion EUR

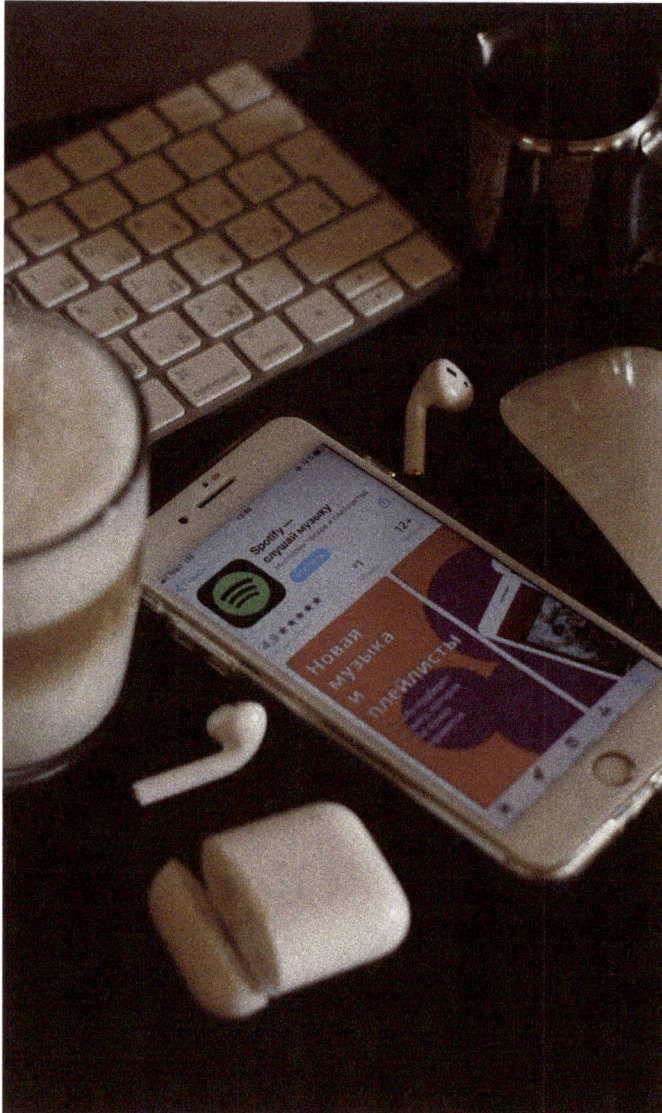

# 92

## Music for every one

Brand: Spotify
Sector: Digital Music Streaming
Market cap: $48.55 Billion

*Courtesy of Matheus Triaquim*

*"Live to ride, ride to live."*

# 93

## Screw It Let`s Ride

Brand: Harley-Davidson
Sector: Premium Motorcycle Manufacturer
Market cap: $5.27 Billion

# 94 The name speaks for itself

Brand: Burberry
Sector: Luxury Fashion and Apparel
Brand value: 6.4 billion U.S. dollars
Market cap: 4.77 Billion GBP

Iconic British Luxury

# PRADA

## MILANO

### DAL 1913

**95** **Be seen, be heard**

Brand: Prada
Sector: Luxury Fashion and Apparel
Brand value: 7.32 billion U.S. dollars
Market cap: 135.62 Billion HKD

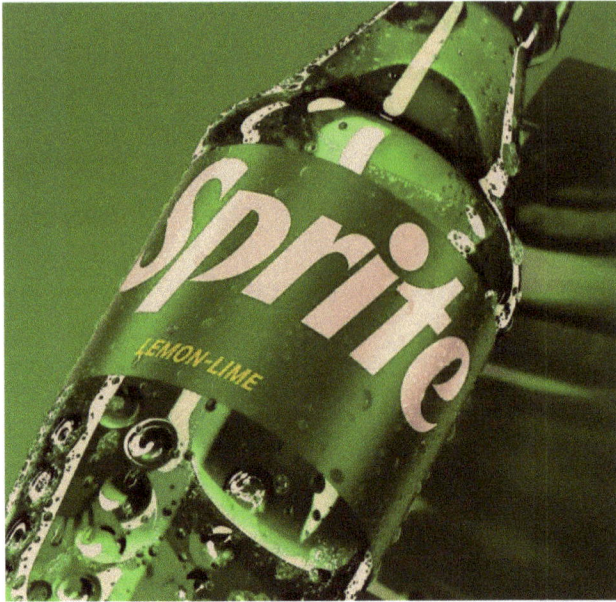

Freedom From Thirst

# 96
## Obey your thirst

Brand: Sprite
Sector: Beverage and Soft Drinks
Brand value: 5 billion U.S. dollars

# 97
## Keep Walking

Brand: Johnnie Walker
Sector: Alcohol (Whisky and Spirits industry)
Brand value: 10.9 billion U.S. dollars

# 98 Those who never stop

Brand: Hennessy
Sector: Alcohol (Cognacs)
Brand value: 5.2 billion U.S. dollars

Courtesy of Per Waernbörg

*Play it Loud*

# 99

## Now you're playing with power!

Brand: Nintendo
Sector: Gaming and Entertainment
Brand value: 8.8 billion U.S. dollars
Market cap: 11.52 Trillion JPY

# 100

Brand: Tesla
Sector: Automotive, Software, and Energy
Brand value: 67.66 billion U.S. dollars
Market cap: $626.54 Billion

No Slogan

*Courtesy of Roberto Nickson*

# 101

## See what`s next

Brand: Netflix
Sector: Motion Picture, Video & TV
Brand value: 24.1 billion U.S. dollars
Market cap: $252.07 Billion

$$-\overset{\text{F}}{\underset{\text{M}}{\times}}-$$

www.ingramcontent.com/pod-product-compliance
Lightning Source LLC
Chambersburg PA
CBHW060926210326
41597CB00042B/4609